W9-BFW-362

741.5
How

County $16.96

Penworthy

10-26-07

© 2007 Viacom International Inc.
All rights reserved. Nickelodeon, NICKELODEON AVATAR: THE LAST AIRBENDER
and all related titles, logos, and characters are trademarks of Viacom International Inc.

131215   How to draw Nickelodeon Avatar . . .

AVATAR CHARACTER SIZE CHART

When drawing, it's important to understand a character's proportions (the correct size of things compared with other things). Cartoon characters are often measured in "heads." For example, Aang is about 5 1/2 heads tall. Use this height chart to help you draw the characters' proportions correctly. Each lined section of this chart is one Aang head high.

13

12

11

10

9

8

7

6

5

4

3

2

1

0

4   Appa   Momo   Toph

HOW TO USE THIS BOOK

You can draw any of the characters in this book by following these simple steps.

Step 1
Start your drawing in the middle of the paper so you won't run out of room.

Step 2
Each new step appears in blue, so you'll always know what to draw next.

Step 3
Take your time and copy the blue lines.

Step 4
Refine the lines of your drawing. Then add the details.

Step 5
Darken the lines you want to keep and erase the rest.

Step 6
Add color to your drawing with colored pencils, markers, paints, or crayons!

AANG

Aang is an adventurous, free-spirited 12-year-old and the only known survivor of the Air Nomads. As the last Airbender, Aang is destined to become the Avatar. His connection to animals and nature allows him to "listen" to the spirits around him as they guide him on his quest to bring good to the world.

Start with a basic circle for Aang's head Then add guidelines for his facial features. Next draw a curved line for his spine.

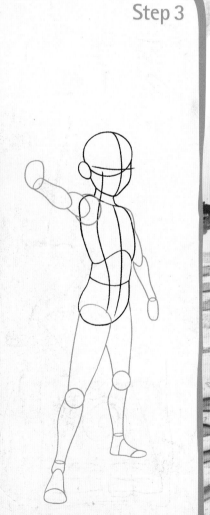

Step 3

Step 4

Step 5

Add Aang's arms, with the right arm raised so the hand and ear are the same level. Then add his legs and feet. Just follow the blue lines!

Now draw Aang's clothing. Then add his eyes, eyebrows, nose, mouth, and the arrow on his forehead. Begin sketching the staff in his right hand.

Next draw Aang's hands and fingers. Add curving lines to his shirt and shorts to show movement and texture. Detail his face by thickening his eyebrows and finishing his eyes. Then add the lines in his ear.

Airbending

Airbenders are faster than other benders because they have air on their side. By controlling the air, Airbenders can run up walls, jump high, and even float for a few seconds. Some airbenders carry a staff, which doesn't hold any magical powers on its own, but it does enhance the power of attacks for the bender.

Earthbending

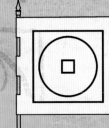

Earthbenders use the earth as their weapon by causing earthquakes, creating crevices in the ground, and raising slabs of stone for defense. Earthbenders also have the power to climb walls and cliffs by manipulating the ground beneath them like an elevator.

ABOUT AVATAR

In a far-off place, there reside four noble Nations: Water, Fire, Earth, and Air. In every nation there are "benders" who are able to control the elements. Power is spread equally among each nation, but only one bender can master all four elements and maintain world order and balance: the Avatar.

Waterbending

A Waterbender's strength comes from his or her ability to manipulate water as a way to control an opponent. Given the ability to suspend water, Waterbenders can build a shield around their position during a fight or to escape an attacker.

Firebending

Firebenders use kicks and jabs to produce surges of flames and fireballs to defeat their enemies. Although aggressive, the Firebender doesn't attack right away. Instead, he or she pursues prey in search of a weakness— once that weakness is discovered, the Firebender strikes.

Aang

Katara

Sokka

Zuko

Princess Azula

Uncle Iroh

Jet

Roku

HOW TO DRAW

NICKELODEON

降击神通

AVATAR

THE LAST AIRBENDER™

Learn to draw all your favorite *Avatar: The Last Airbender* characters.

Illustrated by Shane L. Johnson

TOOLS AND MATERIALS

You'll need to gather a few simple drawing tools before you begin. Start with a regular pencil and eraser so you easily can erase any mistakes. Make sure you have a sharpener and ruler, too. To add color to your drawings, grab some markers, colored pencils, crayons, or even acrylic or watercolor paint.

Paintbrush

Drawing pencil

Paint

Sharpener

Colored pencils

Eraser

Broad-tip markers

Fine-line marker

Step 2

Extend Aang's face, and add his ear and neck; then sketch the basic shape of the torso. Make sure his right shoulder is slightly higher than his left.

Step 6

Carefully erase any stray pencil lines. Darken the outline with a fine-tip black marker or the sharp point of your pencil. Then add vibrant color to give Aang life.

Arrow extends all the way down the back of his head (and down his back!)

Arrows on back of hands

Yes! Eyes are wide open—not droopy

APPA

A giant Sky Bison that was frozen, along with Aang, in an iceberg for 100 years, Appa has the ability to fly. He often transports Aang, Katara, and Sokka on their adventures.

Step 1

Begin by drawing a circle for Appa's head. Then add guidelines to help you draw the facial features. Next draw a curved line to indicate Appa's spine.

Step 2

Add a large oval shape for the upper portion of the body. Draw another sloped half circle for the lower body. Then add the rounded tail.

Step 3

Follow the blue lines to draw Appa's legs and paws. Then extend his head slightly by adding a crescent shape for his chin. Add guidelines for his eyes and nose.

Step 4

Draw the facial details, including his eyes, nose, and tongue. Add a horn on each side of his head. Next draw the details on his paws.

Step 5

Add texture to Appa's fur by drawing short, jagged lines at the edges of his legs and right above his eyes. Draw an arrow on top of his head; then follow the blue lines to add the remaining details.

Step 6

Erase any unnecessary pencil lines. Now add Appa's neutral colors—don't forget his bright pink tongue.

Normal eye

When eye is wide open, a bit of white shows

Eye almost closed

Paws have three toes

MOMO

Momo is Aang's beloved pet, a flying lemur. Remarkably intelligent, he is a helpful addition to Aang's circle of friends. Momo's keen sense of smell and heightened hearing alert Momo of trouble when it is still miles away.

Step 1

Start your drawing by sketching in Momo's head. Use a curved line to reflect the shape of his spine. Then add a horizontal guideline for his face.

Step 2

Next draw the basic shape of Momo's body. Just copy the blue lines!

Step 3

Draw Momo's front and back legs, but be sure to keep him in a squatting position. Extend the face and add a few more guidelines, as shown in blue.

Step 4

Draw two large ears and indicate the inside of his right ear. Then use the guidelines to add two circles for his eyes and nose. Then draw his long, curvy tail.

Step 5

Add details to the inside of the ear and to the eyes. Add his mouth, and refine the fingers. Then draw choppy lines under the ears and on top of his legs to show a furry texture. Create two rings at the tip of his tail.

Step 6

Now clean up your drawing and refine the lines. Grab some markers or crayons and give Momo color. Remember to give him bright green eyes.

Momo has wings

Yes! Eyes are slightly oval shaped

No! Eyes not too circular

Feet light on top . . .

Head is shaped like a stop sign

. . . dark on bottom

KATARA

Despite losing her mother at a young age, Katara has grown up to become a caring and passionate young woman. Her kindness is apparent in all aspects of her life, especially in her desire to save her tribe by becoming a Master Waterbender. Katara always wears her mother's necklace as a reminder of her mother's goodwill and loving spirit.

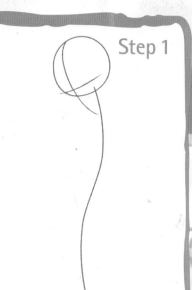

Step 1

To draw Katara, begin with a basic circle for her head. Add facial guidelines and a curved line for her spine.

Step 3

Follow the blue lines to add her arms, legs, and feet.

Step 4

Now go ahead and draw Katara's dress and the fur on her boots. Then add her eyes, nose, mouth, and long braid.

Step 5

Finish her dress and shoes. Add details to her hair, face, and hand. Then draw her choker.

Step 2

Extend the face and add her ear. Now draw the outline of her torso, following the curve of the guideline from step 1.

Step 6

Carefully erase any stray pencil lines. Then use color to dress Katara in royal blues. Her eyes match her dress!

Thick eyelash line

Eye shape is feminine

Hair pieces from front of head attach to the bun at back of head

Braid has eight bumps

SOKKA

Katara's brother, Sokka, is a loyal friend. Although he can be stubborn, his strength and determination are clearly visible in his actions and behavior toward others. He is practical, preferring the physical world to the spiritual, and would rather practice throwing his prized boomerang than waterbending.

Step 1

After drawing the circle, add the guidelines for Sokka's head and body.

Step 3

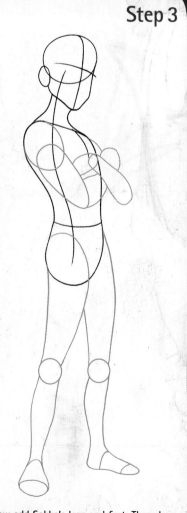

Now add Sokka's legs and feet. Then draw his arms—notice how his left arm crosses over his right arm.

Step 4

Draw his heavy overcoat, pants, and boots. Add the boomerang in his right hand, and draw his facial features and hair.

Step 5

Follow the blue lines to create texture on the coat and boots. Finish the details on the boomerang and on his face.

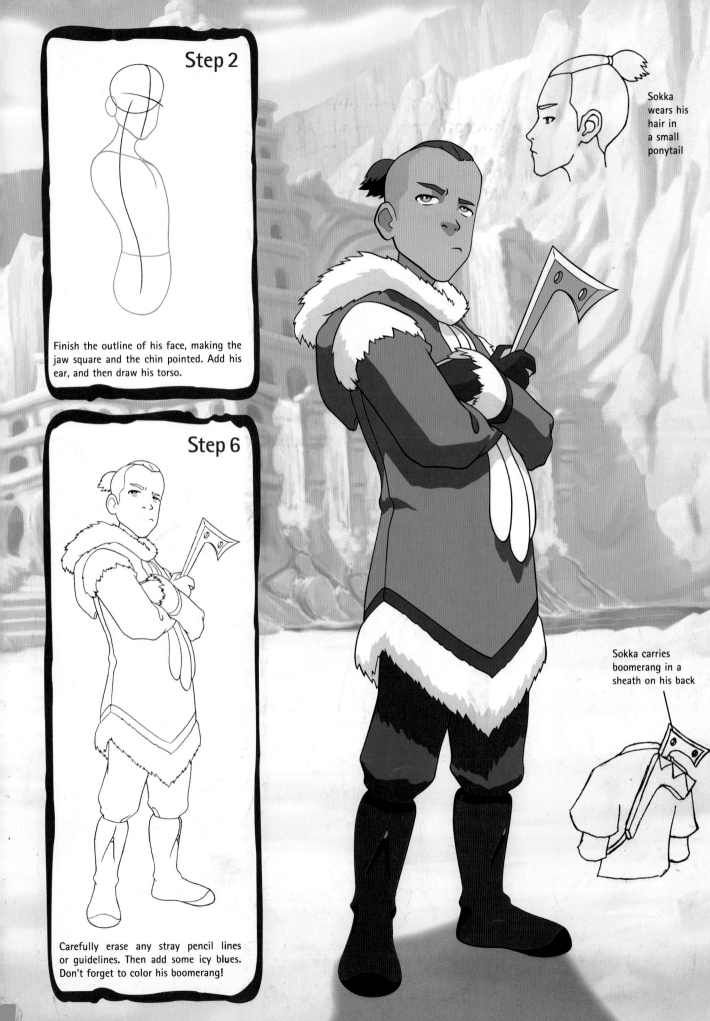

Step 2

Finish the outline of his face, making the jaw square and the chin pointed. Add his ear, and then draw his torso.

Step 6

Carefully erase any stray pencil lines or guidelines. Then add some icy blues. Don't forget to color his boomerang!

Sokka wears his hair in a small ponytail

Sokka carries boomerang in a sheath on his back

PRINCE ZUKO

Banished from his homeland by his father, Fire Lord Ozai, Prince Zuko is an extremely determined teenager on a journey to regain his title and throne. But in order to do so, he must capture the Avatar. A skilled Firebender, Zuko's overzealous attitude and haughty manner are his greatest flaws.

Step 1

Begin Prince Zuko by drawing a circle for his head and a slightly curved line for his spine. Add the facial guidelines.

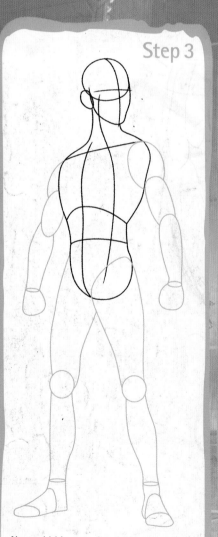

Step 3

Next add his arms, hands, legs, and feet. Just copy the blue lines.

Step 4

Draw his clothes; then add his facial features and ponytail. Take your time, and follow the blue lines.

Step 5

Define Prince Zuko's armor by drawing details. Then add the finishing touches to his fingers, ear, and face.

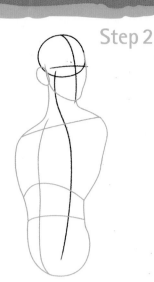

Step 2

Extend the face and add his right ear. Then draw his torso, adding more guidelines.

Step 6

Carefully erase all of the guidelines you don't need. Then darken the lines you want to keep and use black, red, gray, and brown to color him.

Hair is shaved into a diamond shape

Left ear is disfigured

Zuko can't open his left eye much wider than this because the eye is damaged

Abingdon Elementary School Library
Abingdon, Virginia

JET

Jet is a teenage vigilante with a deep-seated grudge against the Fire Nation for killing his parents when he was a young boy. As the leader of a group of Earth Kingdom children called "The Freedom Fighters," Jet antagonizes the Fire Nation soldiers every chance he gets.

Step 1

Start by drawing a circle for Jet's head and guidelines for his face. Then draw a slightly curved line for his spine.

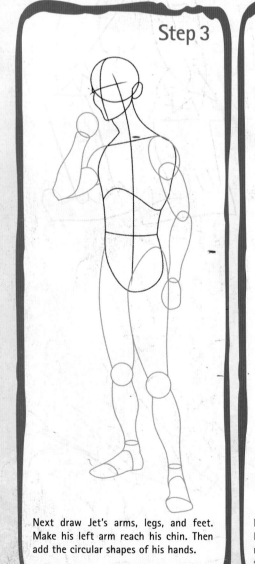

Step 3

Next draw Jet's arms, legs, and feet. Make his left arm reach his chin. Then add the circular shapes of his hands.

Step 4

Draw his outfit by following the blue lines. Add his shaggy hair and his eyes, nose, and mouth. Then draw a wavy line from his mouth.

Step 5

Now refine your drawing by adding all of the small details. Pay close attention to his boots, shirt, and hair.

Step 2

Add the lower portion of his face and his left ear. Then sketch the basic shape of his torso.

Step 6

Erase any extra pencil lines. Then trace over your drawing with a fine-tip black marker. Now add bright color.

Eyes are long and almond shaped; eyebrows are thin and expressive

Jet's thick, shaggy hair covers his forehead

UNCLE IROH

Zuko's Uncle Iroh was a commander of the Fire Nation. Since Zuko's banishment, Uncle Iroh has been training his nephew, teaching him new Firebending skills and preparing him for his inevitable battle with the Avatar.

Step 1

Draw a circle for the head and a curved line for the spine. Then add the facial guidelines.

Step 3

Next draw Uncle Iroh's legs and feet. Add his arms, making sure they are folded behind his back.

Step 4

Follow the blue lines to outline his cloak. Draw his eyes, nose, and mouth. Then add his hair and beard.

Step 5

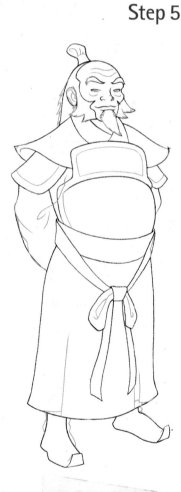

Now add crease lines to his cloak. Detail his face by adding wrinkles, and touch up his hair and beard.

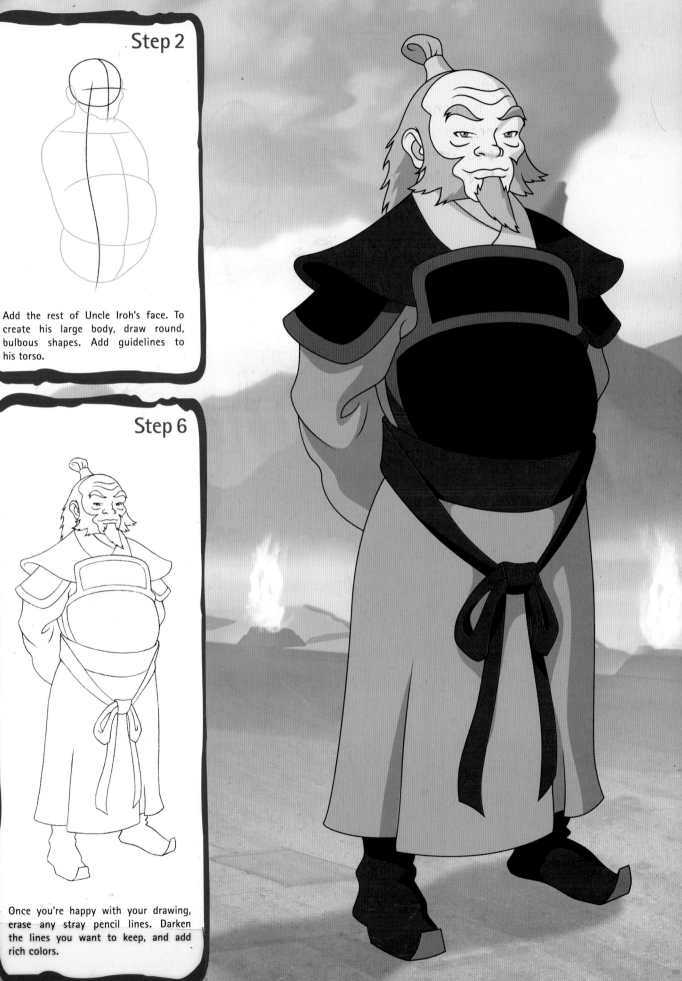

Step 2

Add the rest of Uncle Iroh's face. To create his large body, draw round, bulbous shapes. Add guidelines to his torso.

Step 6

Once you're happy with your drawing, erase any stray pencil lines. Darken the lines you want to keep, and add rich colors.

23

AVATAR ROKU

Roku is Aang's Avatar predecessor. A Firebender by birth, Roku's benign spirit is evidence that not all Firebenders are evil. He now serves as Aang's protector, offering guidance and wisdom to the young Avatar.

Step 1

Start with the head, and then add guide-lines. For this straight-on view, you may want to use a ruler to draw the spine.

Step 3

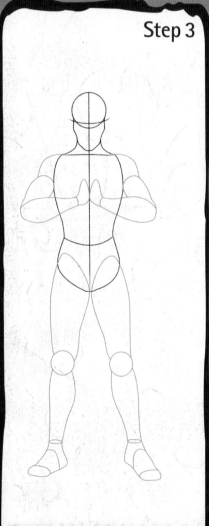

Complete Roku's body by drawing his legs, arms, and feet. Notice how his hands meet at the center of his chest.

Step 4

Use the blue lines as a guide to draw his robe—or try tracing them. Add his facial details, hair, beard, and headpiece.

Step 5

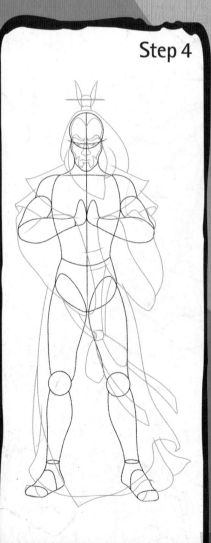

Use curving lines to add movement to his robe. Finish drawing his hands, and use jagged lines to add texture to his hair.

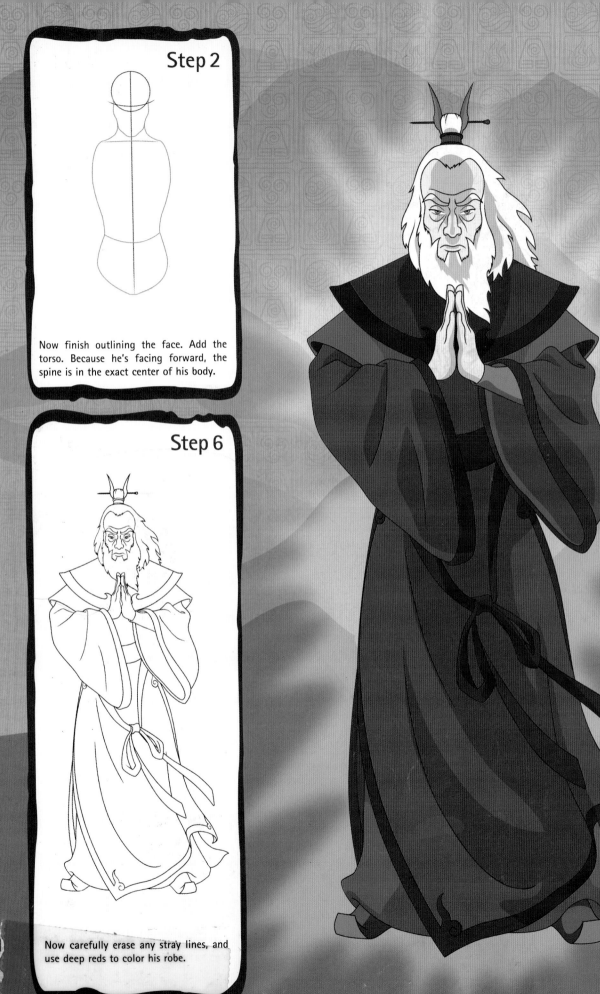

Step 2

Now finish outlining the face. Add the torso. Because he's facing forward, the spine is in the exact center of his body.

Step 6

Now carefully erase any stray lines, and use deep reds to color his robe.

PRINCESS AZULA

Like her older brother, Prince Zuko, Princess Azula is a perfectionist. A Firebending prodigy, Azula is the favored child of Fire Lord Ozai and is strongly resented by Zuko. She enjoys tormenting her brother, taking pleasure in his current exile. Her vindictive and ruthless demeanor is cause for alarm to all those with whom she comes in contact.

Step 1

To draw Princess Azula, begin by drawing a circle for her head. Then add guidelines.

Step 3

Add Azula's legs, keeping her right leg bent at the knee and her left leg outstretched. Next draw her arms.

Step 4

Draw Azula's eyes, nose, and mouth. Add her hair and headpiece. Then draw her garb, and add pointed ends to her shoes.

Step 5

Fine-tune your drawing by adding details to the shoes, dress, and face. Finish drawing her hands and long fingernails.

Step 2

Now finish outlining her face, and add her ears. Then use the guideline to draw her torso, which is angled to the left.

Step 6

Clean up your drawing by erasing any extra pencil lines. Then add color to finish Princess Azula.

Metal ring

Metal piece "folds" down the center

Azula's hairpiece is made of metal

Fingers are long and slender with pointed nails

TOPH

Although she is blind, Toph is a powerful and highly skilled Earthbender. Because of her heightened senses and innate connection to the earth, she is the undefeated Earthbending champion— the perfect person to teach Aang her art.

Step 1

Start by drawing a circle for Toph's head. Add guidelines for her head and spine.

Step 3

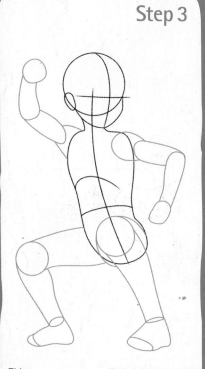

This pose may seem a little tricky, but it's really not. Draw her legs, bending them at the knee. Add her arms and feet.

Step 4

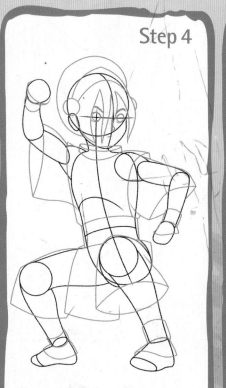

Follow the blue lines to draw Toph's shorts, shirt, and belt. Then draw her wispy hair and the facial details.

Step 5

Draw her fingers and toes. Next add the finishing touches, such as the buttons, wrist cuffs, and hair details.

Step 2

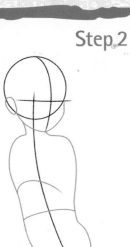

Draw her rounded jaw and ear. Then add her torso, curving it slightly to the right. Add guidelines to the torso.

Yes! Eyes always "look" straight ahead

No! Eyes never "look" up/down/ left/right

Yes! Eye does not have a highlight

No!

Step 6

Clean up your drawing and give Toph's clothing bright yellows and greens. Color her misty blue eyes.

TUI AND LA

Tui and La are spirits that have crossed over into the mortal world in the form of koi fish. Tui is a moon spirit from which Waterbenders draw their power. La, the spirit of the ocean, is greatly appreciated and idolized by the Water Tribe. Both Tui and La swim freely inside the secret gardens of the Northern Water Tribe.

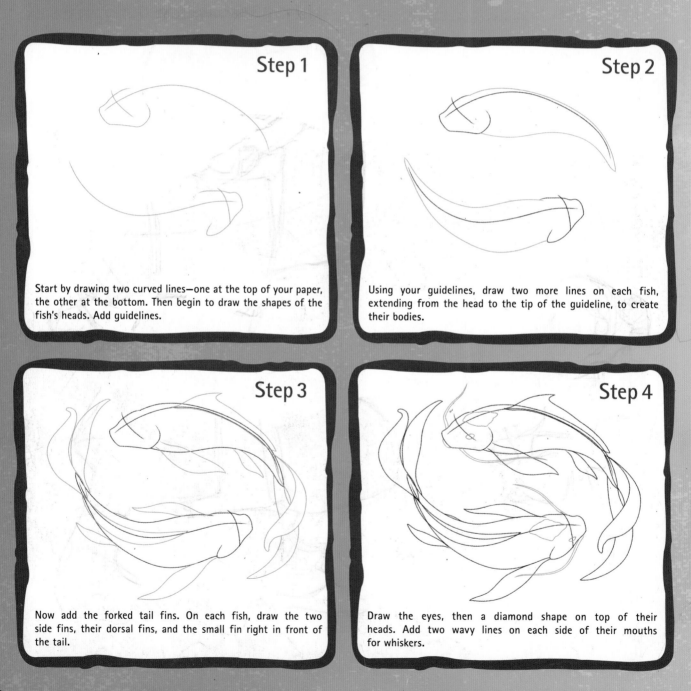

Step 1

Start by drawing two curved lines—one at the top of your paper, the other at the bottom. Then begin to draw the shapes of the fish's heads. Add guidelines.

Step 2

Using your guidelines, draw two more lines on each fish, extending from the head to the tip of the guideline, to create their bodies.

Step 3

Now add the forked tail fins. On each fish, draw the two side fins, their dorsal fins, and the small fin right in front of the tail.

Step 4

Draw the eyes, then a diamond shape on top of their heads. Add two wavy lines on each side of their mouths for whiskers.

Step 5

Finish drawing each fish's eye. Refine your drawing by adding details to the fins. Just copy the blue lines.

Step 6

Erase any extra guidelines. Darken your drawing with a fine-tip black marker. Then add blues and purples.

UNTIL NEXT TIME...

Now that you know how to draw Aang and his friends, use your imagination to put your artwork to good use. Make your own storybooks, postcards, bookplates, wrapping paper, greeting cards, or posters—just keep creating works of art!